STEEL-BELTED *GRIMM*

by MIKE PETERS

Starring Mother Goose & Grimm

TOPPER BOOKS

AN IMPRINT OF PHAROS BOOKS • A SCRIPPS HOWARD COMPANY

NEW YORK

Library of Congress Catalog Card Number: 88-60374

Pharos ISBN: 0-88687-366-5

Printed in the United States of America

Topper Books
An Imprint of Pharos Books
A Scripps Howard Company
200 Park Avenue
New York, NY 10166

10 9 8 7 6 5 4 3 2 1

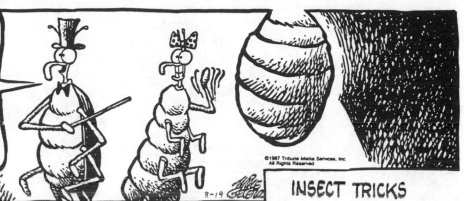

"AND NOW MY LOVELY ASSISTANT WILL ENTER THE COCOON... NOTICE SHE HAS NO WINGS.

©1987 Tribune Media Services, Inc.
All Rights Reserved

8-19

INSECT TRICKS

TSK, TSK, AMY... YOU HAVEN'T BEEN USING THOSE LITTLE BIRDS TO CLEAN BETWEEN YOUR TEETH AGAIN...

©1987 Tribune Media Services, Inc.
All Rights Reserved

IF A MIME FALLS IN AN EMPTY FOREST DOES IT MAKE A SOUND?

the NEWS

HUEY, DEWEY AND LOUIE

GRIMMY... I DECIDED IT'S TIME I GOT YOU A PET.

OH BOY, YOU MEAN A DOG?

5-30

WAIT HERE.

REALLY? A DOG? YOU GOT ME A DOG?...A REAL DOG?

A SMALL, WET, SLIMY DOG.

I WANTED A DOG...BUT SHE GOT ME A FISH.

A COLD, YUCKY, FISH...!

31

A STUPID, COLD, YUCKY FISH.

I'LL CALL HIM LASSIE.

WHISTLER'S MOTHER-IN-LAW

WHENEVER GEORGE COMES INTO A SINGLES BAR... HE ALWAYS SECRETLY REMOVES THE RING IN HIS NOSE.

I'VE FALLEN IN LOVE WITH A SIX-PIECE DINING ROOM SET.

UGH.... UMPH

SUMO CHESS

OH, OH... I'M LOST, I DON'T REMEMBER HOW TO GET HOME.

I'M GOING TO BE FORCED TO LIVE ON THE STREET,, TO SLEEP IN DARK ALLEYS...

AND EAT GARBAGE OUT OF FILTHY TRASH CANS.

HEY... I COULD GET IN TO THIS...

11-23

WHAT'S SO BAD ABOUT LIVING ON THE STREET?

IT'S JUST LIKE LIVING AT HOME, THE GROUND IS MY CARPET...

AND THE SKY IS MY ROOF...

MY ROOF'S LEAKING.

11-24

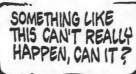

GEE...I'D REALLY LIKE TO COME TO THE CHURCH SOCIAL TONIGHT...

BUT I'M JUST SITTING DOWN TO A SEVEN-COURSE MEAL...

A PIZZA AND A SIX-PACK.

LOOK, GRIMMY...IT'S A BENJI MOVIE, ISN'T HE THE SWEETEST LITTLE THING?

"SO CUTE AND ADORABLE, DO YOU WANT ANYTHING BEFORE IT STARTS?

AN INSULIN SHOT.

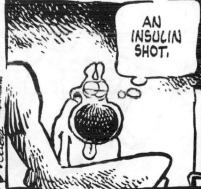

FORTY-SEVEN,
FORTY-EIGHT,
FORTY-NINE,
FIFTY...
FIFTY-ONE...

SUDDENLY.. WITHOUT A WORD... MARGE AND ALDO REALIZED THE MAGIC HAD GONE OUT OF THEIR MARRIAGE.

MR. POTATO PANCAKE

OK, WHICH TRASH CAN SHALL WE OPEN TODAY?

TRASH CAN NUMBER ONE...

..NUMBER TWO, OR NUMBER THREE?

SUDDENLY I FEEL LIKE MONTY HALL.

2-25

STRANGE...THIS DOG FOOD IS FIZZING.

GRIMM...YOU PUT PERRIER WATER IN YOUR GRAVY TRAIN!

I'M JUST AN '80'S KIND OF GUY.

GRIM

2-21

WHERE HAVE YOU BEEN ALL NIGHT? AND WIPE THAT SMILE OFF YOUR FACE...

WHAT'S WRONG WITH YOU... CAT GOT YOUR TONGUE?

GRIMM.. GET OFF THE SOFA.

DOGS AREN'T SUPPOSED TO BE ON THE SOFA.

WHAT? HUH?

SURELY THERE MUST BE SOME MISTAKE, OH NO, DEAR GOD, IT'S TRUE....

3-14

I AM A DOG.

ALL THIS TIME I'VE BEEN A DOG AND DIDN'T KNOW IT.

3-15

SO THAT EXPLAINS WHY I'M COVERED IN FUR AND I EAT OFF THE FLOOR.

I JUST THOUGHT I WAS AN UGLY KID WITH HYGIENE PROBLEMS.

GRIMMY... RISE AND SHINE.

SINK AND RUST.

FETCH, GRIMMY.

OH, I GET IT.. I'M A DOG, SO YOU THROW THE STICK AND I KEEP BRINGING IT BACK TO YOU, RIGHT?

BOY, OH BOY, DOES THIS SOUND LIKE A FUN-FILLED AFTERNOON.

THESE THINGS TAKE TIME.

10-3

THERE IS A GOD.

HA-WHOA GRIMMY POO.

HOW'S MUMMY'S WIDOW BABY, THIS MORNING?

DID HIM SWEEP-O-TAY WAST NITE? HUH, DID HIM?

WHY DOES SHE DO THIS TO ME ON AN EMPTY STOMACH?

SAY... COME TO THINK OF IT... MINE HASN'T BROUGHT ME ANY LUCK EITHER...

SEX ED.

THERE'S NO REASON TO BE AFRAID OF ME, ATTILA.

MY BARK IS WORSE THAN MY BITE.

BARK

SEE?

10-20

F.R

LOOK, GRIMMY...

I PICKED UP A TREE ON MY WAY HOME.

I LOVE THIS WOMAN.

12/22

MARINE BIOLOGISTS

SHAMU THE KILLER WHALE

DOGS LIKE TO FIND A NICE COOL PLACE TO SIT ON A SUMMER AFTERNOON...

I PREFER JELL-O.

HMM... DOG TRICKS.

DOG TRICKS

LAY

DOG TRICKS

I COULD GET INTO THIS.

HA-WOE, MY WIDOW WASCAL, IS HIM TARVING?

IS HIM WEO-WEE, WEO-WEE HUNGWEE?

SHE WANTS TO KNOW IF YOU'D LIKE DINNER.

I SPEAK ELMER FUDD.

HA-WOE, PUDDY TAT, IS HIM MUMMY'S WIDOW BOO BOO?

MUMMY WUVS YOU.

C'MON UP ON MUMMY'S WAP... WAP, WAP, WAP WAP, WAP...

FRIGHTENING, ISN'T IT?

Panel 1: WOULD PUDDY TAT AND PUPPY DOG WIKE TO PWAY?

Panel 2: HUH? WOULD YOU WIKE TO PWAY WIF MOMMY?

Panel 3: MOMMY WUVS TO PWAY...

Panel 4: HUMOR HER, I'LL GO GET HELP...

Panel 5: GWIMMY POO, GWIMMY POO.

Panel 6: DOES HIM WANT TUM NUM-NUMS? GOOD NUMMIES FOR THE TUMMIES?

Panel 8: THE LEGS GO NEXT.

5-18
5-19

WHAT'S WONG, GWIMMY? YOU WOOK TICK.

OOOOOOH... IS MY WIDOW BABY TICK?

IS HIM WEO-WEE, WEO-WEE TICK?

NO, BUT HIM GOING TO BE TICK...

DOCTOR... POOR WIDOW GRIMMY-POO IS TICK.

HIM EAT BAD NUMMIES.

NOW HIM ALL TICK TO HIS TUM-TUM.

CAN YOU MAKE HER TALK NORMAL AGAIN, DOC?

I'VE BEEN LYING HERE THREE HOURS AND NOT ONE PERSON HAS OFFERED MOUTH TO MOUTH.

3-19

LOOK AT THIS BANK STATEMENT!

I CAN'T BE OVERDRAWN...

I STILL HAVE __TWO__ CHECKS LEFT.

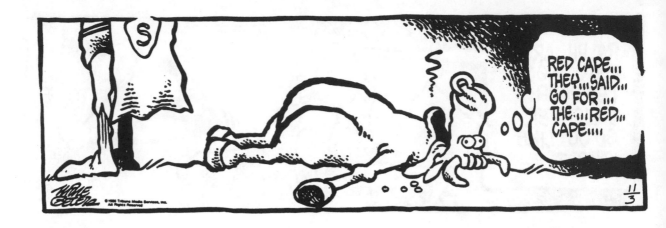

HE FELL FOR THE OLD CATNIP IN THE COPIER TRICK.

©1987 Tribune Media Services, Inc.
All Rights Reserved

11-30

OH, POOR GRIMMY GOT HIMSELF A BAD COLD...

A HOT BOWL OF SOUP WILL MAKE HIM FEEL A LOT BETTER.

SHE'S RIGHT.

5-9

WINNIE THE PUNK

REMEMBER, MARCH IS THE BEGINNING OF FLEA AND TICK SEASON...

THEEEEEY'RE BAAAAACK.

3-17

©1987 Tribune Media Services, Inc.
All Rights Reserved

HE FOUND SOME JUNK BONDS.

12-17

DO YOU MIND?... AFTER ALL, THAT WAS MY AUNT HARRIET.

I HATE WHEN YOU START CURLING UP WITH A GOOD BOOK...

WHOA... I DON'T BELIEVE IT... I FINALLY CAUGHT MY TAIL.

I'LL HAVE IT STUFFED AND MOUNTED ON A BIG WOODEN PLAQUE...

AND THEN I'LL HANG IT OVER THE FIREPLA...

WHAT AM I SAYING?

SSSSSSS WHIZZZZZ

I CAN'T BELIEVE IT. AFTER ALL THESE YEARS I FINALLY CAUGHT MY TAIL....

I WONDER HOW I DID IT? EITHER I'M GETTING FASTER...

OR MY TAIL IS GETTING SLOWER.

DEAR MZ. GOOSE, IS IT TRUE THAT DOGS CAN SMELL OVER 50 MILES AWAY?

YES... ESPECIALLY IF THEY'RE WET.

OH BOY... A PIECE OF GUM STUCK UNDER THE TABLE.

I WONDER WHAT KIND IT IS?

A WOP BOPA LU BOP A WOMP BAM BOOM

TUTTI-FRUTTI.

AH CHOOO

WHAT'S WRONG WITH ME? WHY DO I KEEP SNEEZING?

OH OH...

WHAT IF I'M ALLERGIC TO DOGS?

MZ. GOOSE... COULD YOU TAKE CARE OF MY GERMAN SHEPHERD FOR A FEW DAYS?

SURE.

ALL I SAID WAS I WAS A VET...

YOU LOCKED THE DOGGY DOOR AGAIN.

STRIP POKER

2-24

GATORADE 5¢

© 1992 Tribune Media Services, Inc.
All Rights Reserved

6-15

PSST...009,
I THINK
SOMEBODY
SLIPPED YOU
A MICKEY.

© 1987 Tribune Media Services, Inc.
All Rights Reserved

OH, BOY... IT'S MY FAVORITE TV SHOW, CARL THE WONDER POODLE.

IN THIS EPISODE HE ACCIDENTALLY SWALLOWS HIS SQUEAK TOY.

AND NOW HE'S TRYING TO DO THE HEIMLICH MANEUVER ON HIMSELF...

7-11

© 1988 Tribune Media Services, Inc.
All Rights Reserved

SOMETIMES CARL IS A DORK.

I ENJOY WATCHING CARL THE WONDER POODLE.

HIS STORIES ARE ALWAYS SO BELIEVABLE.

TODAY CARL IS TUNNELING INTO A SAC BASE TO DEFUSE A MALFUNCTIONING M-X MISSILE...

© 1988 Tribune Media Services, Inc.
All Rights Reserved

I BELIEVE IT, REALLY, I BELIEVE IT.

7-12

OH-OH... CARL THE WONDER POODLE IS REALLY IN TROUBLE THIS TIME...

IT'S THE MORNING OF THE BIG DOG SHOW...

AND ONE OF THE RHINESTONES FELL OUT OF HIS STERLING SILVER DOGGIE COLLAR.

COULDN'T YOU JUST DIE?

GRIMMY... YOU'VE GOT TO DO MORE WITH YOUR MIND THAN JUST WATCHING TV...

BUT I DO... I ALWAYS MAKE SURE I READ ONE BOOK A WEEK.

TV GUIDE

CHAIN SAW OUT OF GAS, HUH? SURE...I'LL FILL IT FOR YOU...

HERB'S LAST SALE

9-8

OF COURSE I'M PUTTING HORSERADISH ON MY DOG FOOD... AFTER ALL, WHAT IS DOG FOOD?..IT'S HORSE...RIGHT?

TV

DOG COMMERCIALS

11-21

MR. ROGERS NEIGHBORHOOD WATCH

FLEAS 'Я' US...

3-27

LOOK OUT!

I'M OFF TO A T.G.I.T. PARTY...

THANK GOD IT'S TRASH DAY.

3-29

IF CORN BREAD IS MADE FROM CORN...

AND CHEESECAKE IS MADE FROM CHEESE...

WHAT ARE DOG BISCUITS MADE FROM?

I CAN'T WAIT TO GET HOME...

...AND GO TO SLEEP ON MY NICE, SOFT, WARM, DOWN-FILLED PILLOW.